WHAT
THE NIGHT
NUMBERED

Also by Bradford Tice

Rare Earth
(New Rivers Press)

WHAT THE NIGHT NUMBERED

Poems by Bradford Tice

Winner of the 2014 Trio Award

Tice, Bradford
1st edition.

ISBN: 978-0-9855292-8-4
Library of Congress Control Number: 2014954704

Interior Layout by Lea C. Deschenes
Cover Design by Dorinda Wegener
Cover Art by Ronnie Beets
Editing by Matt Mauch and Sara Lefsyk

Printed in Tennessee, USA
Trio House Press, Inc.
Ponte Vedra Beach, FL

To contact the author, send an email to tayveneese@comcast.net

*This book is dedicated to the histories
we are not taught, but discover along the way.*

And to the Stonewall girls...

TABLE OF CONTENTS

I.

II.

"We are the Stonewall girls!
We wear our hair in curls
We don't wear underwear
We show our pubic hairs."

I.

Two Falsehoods

I. Fiddle or Lyre

My grandmother once said, "A story is a lie
with legs," meaning the good ones
have to strut. Picture the tale of Nero

fiddling as Rome burned, the bow sawing
at the strings like a wartime surgeon.
Nevermind that the fiddle was 1,600 years

premature in its invention. A lyre then.
A lute. What do the details matter regarding
such ecstatic footwork at the fall of an empire?

II. Fiddle and a Liar

Take the Stonewall, the Riots, that hot
summer night in '69 when drag queens
in calf-high patent leather boots, mop-tops

and hot pants formed a can-can line,
high-kicked the police into submission.
Gay power is born! Lies, all lies, they say.

This is how it starts, how it goes. Tell me
you love me, and I'll believe you. Tell me you'll
never leave. Tell me the flames licking

the towers are a song you wrote for me,
how all things end in the compass of my face.
Us lovers, we'll swallow anything.

Psyche's First Trial

I.

My grandmother gave me a room,
light-filled, above the front yard, and washed
her hands of it. Although in truth I wasn't
Psyche then. Not yet anything more than a fresh boy
in the dirt who's given packets of seeds,

wisteria   mustard   fennel

the acre parceled. As a child, I was given a task.
How can I explain the burden? Granny's
eyes overcast with cataracts, she gave me
the garden—
                    chafed flecks
of a splintered field—each seed with its kind.
At the scarred kitchen table, I sorted
them by piles,

feverfew   soapwort   sea lavender

and through them, ants marched like calamity,
an invasion that never desisted. I wondered,
broken down, what the earth numbered.
Look close enough and you can always find
the aberration—core without husk, lone
forager estranged from the path in search
of the cleft through which it entered.

carob   acorn   almond

On that Midwestern farm, field dirt
tinted the wind. There
were voices—shouts called across
pasture, echoes from the well,
                              soothing and soporific.
Voices so unlike
the ones I was sent from.
My father never liked things underfoot,
so Mama packed a suitcase, her lipstick
a violet on my cheek, sent me away.

I spent a year with Granny.
Hard frost, a month of rain,
and then life suckled from the softened
earth. Granny kept
                    to her plot.

The sheeted beds of bulbs like snowbanks,
a massacre of ghosts in the yard—bamboo
teepeed and tied in preparation for the vine—
and the seeding, to which she always returned.

mint   *oat*   *coriander*

There is always a crack to move through.
Granny's hands, neglected leather, stroked the walls.
She moved toward whatever light
was figured.
                    One learns to respect
a well-turned row, the shoulder we take to the plow.
In every pocket—shirt, jeans, socks—
there was a jar,
                    to each was allotted a texture.

grit   *millet*   *kernel*

When I came to the city, burrs stowed away
in the knit, that other farm—my father's farm—
as forgotten as the piles of dirt Mama swept
into the corners of the kitchen, an ash of desperation
piled higher, a burnt-down life.

poppy   *sunflower*   *marigold*

Grounded in the past, ground to dust and silt,
the garden was what I lost.
No longer admitted to that space,
                                with its heavy air.

One reaps what one sows,
or so Granny said, and I have found
no evidence by which
to doubt her.
                Who has not pulled
fruitlessly at the shoots of a garden
gone to seed?

jimson   *cocklebur*   *milkweed*

You get by or you don't. There's not much
more to learn. I haven't seen my grandmother
in over five years, yet when I look
into the mirror, her face, sepia-toned,
stares back. The dime store
wig with its flattened coffee curls, the seam
hidden. Becoming.

sesame   *alfalfa*   *wild flower*

II.

In Central Park, the boys are scattered, weeds
finding root in the gutters, the crevices of bricks.

semen   rubber   rolling papers

I always knew it would come to this.
I left on the night my father caught me
in Mama's wedding dress.

lace   bead pearl   satin

The buckle-end of the belt caught in my back,
and the scars are just twists in an alley—
long coming. Unloosed in the dark,
any baby-faced boy can find a thumb
                                        to nurse.

Age thirteen, my pockets filled with as much
of Mama's makeup as they would carry,
I left my father's house, that coffin,

boarded a bus for New York, the lights
already starting to burn at the edge of the plain.

mascara   soft honey   glitter

I found work as a page to queens,
the drag strip boys with their magic—
into the water closet and *presto*—a softer sex.
My labors, all in preparation for the stroll,
were many.

Here, every diamond
is sham, and how can one not love such
fidelity,

       such rations for the foragers,

pilfered from chinks in the concrete,
from the midnight dresses.

sequin   *gold lamé*   *spangle*

For these lesser forms of life,
there are questions that never get asked.

Even ragweed has its season, its chance to shimmy
open in the wind's coarse hands—
                       the next spell.

The world may think there is no
category, slot, fit for a boy in love with the lick
of glitz, but hooked to the plain as we are,
there is always a grand gesture, a way to thrive.

Suitors Mark the Arrival
of Psyche on Christopher Street

Skin the color of ginger root and honey, he came
       to the street with only the clothes he was wearing,
three quarters and a penny he sucked inside
       his cheek, a torn bus ticket, a split lip,

and his stories. Or his lies as we called them—for how else
       could you describe them, laced and stitched
as they were with the color of a life unsuited
       for ones such as us? To anyone who'd listen,

which is no one we assure you, he talked of the famous
       school he attended in Paris—*L'École des Bêtes.*
On the stairwell of Christopher St. Station,
       his hair intricate curls that twisted into his lashes,

he searched the crowds. Worn and stained, seated
       eye-level to the street, halfway between the over-
and underworld, "Can you believe it?" he said.
       "Alligators and lions?" Speaking of dissection,

lessons a fury of rising pigeons, he described
       the softness of fur, roughness of scales
as knife went in—bone-dust thrown up by the saw's
       teeth on the sternum. "Frogs?!" he said, eyes

skirted with mascara. "The université would not
       allow students to study
on such common life." So he talked of incisions—
       peeling back the small purse of a lion's ear,

the feathery lace of a bull shark's gills. It was all bifid ribs,
        vitreous humour, watching the exposed hearts
of hummingbirds beat a thousand times per minute.
        Once, we laid ourselves in the dark gathered beneath

oaks in Central Park—his spunk drying on the insides
        of our thighs. "You know I tasted one once.
The class had finished dissecting one of the big cats—
        a Bengal. When no one was looking, I sliced

a morsel of its leg. I can't describe it to you—
        mud of a mangrove swamp, boar meat,
sambar, gaur, scent of sun in grasslands.
        And power. Most of all power." We never slept

with him again, though we've felt his passing
        on the corners, a kind of breathlessness. Stories
followed—the Avenue suddenly a village of natives on a hunt
        for ghost-like prints leading into darkness.

The Golden Rats

At this hour, a sparrow shivers under the falling
dew, the night almost done. On the other side
of the Park someone is shooting bottle rockets
and Roman candles, the sizzle of their arc
bright and brief against the sky. Psyche watches
the others: Gin Phizzy, Zazu, Tommy, Martini Angel,
the gang all here. *Why do you call yourself rats?*
Why golden?
                    Because we are glitter washed in the sewers.

A boy in a skinny car touches his cock
through the denim of his jeans. A man groans, wets his lips,
swears he will never do this again. Windows are down
and the boy can smell rain, which reminds him
of a springtime in Missouri, the smell of wild grapes,
cut grass, the septic scent of the runoff behind
his family's home.
                        Across the street, Psyche watches
Zazu watch that car—the two dark heads of the occupants.
At this moment, they both feel older than that need,
older than the dark has grown. Maybe they're
both thinking the boy in that car now hates
a part of himself he was once unafraid to touch.
Maybe they're thinking of another hour late as this,
and of other cars that looked down streets that curved,
split, headed any number of ways.

At an earlier hour, the boy was given the code,
made one of them, his new family
gathered under the awning of a burned out
clothing store. Zazu took a pin and slid it through the lobe
of that boy's ear, threaded the hoop,

the blood bright and brief. She counted out
what they live by: *Be kind to someone every day,*
make sure your makeup's never running…can't be dirty…
protect who's in trouble, attacked, someone queer…
never wear bras or girdles, no leather, fur.
We want nothing dead on you, Bambi.

From the alley Psyche hears a telephone ringing,
no one is picking up, and she knows each of them,
within earshot, pictures someone on the other end
of the line. The other end of a boy touching himself
for what pleasure it earns.
                                        Psyche asks,

What are you watching for?

His baby face, Zazu answers. *When he steps out that car,*
I'll know if he's made it. If he's golden.

A door slams, but Psyche doesn't look.
She already knows that face, can see it jogging back,
grinning to have gone to the end of a thing
and then past it.

PSYCHE AT THE ORACLE

Some nights, I sweat out my dreams and wake thinner—a robin
    pulled down the throat of a serpent, and the syllable
I'm shaping the heft of is *you*. It's always you.
    I picture Mama in that rowboat in the field, capping
on a wave of switchgrass, no sight of water for miles, and you're
    bending toward her, touching the arc of her cheek.
We didn't know it then, but she was already rowing away from us,
    the swell of the meadow drawing her out of herself.
That's how I feel sometimes when I wake in this city
    in the smallest hours of morning, the ghost
of your name a trace in the room. What I've wanted from this life
    is a song with two harmonies, one echoing and amplifying
the other, like a child practicing acoustics in a coatroom.
    Five years, not a word spoken between us.
The reason I left is simple and selfish—I could not place one more
    parcel in that dinghy Mama angled toward abyss—
the vessel you watched until it was folded between
    black night, grass-crest, the broad, yellow faces of sunflowers.
The other night, I woke to the sound of birdwings flailing
    at the glass, and for half an instant, I thought I saw you
seated in the chair in the corner, legs crossed, hand
    on your knee. I wandered down Central.
In back of a boarded-up street fair, I found one of those fortune
    teller machines—chipped gypsy face, hair bound
in a bandanna, hands (one missing a finger) poised over dull
    crystal, as if the future were nothing bright.
Oracle, was it my father wedded me to the cold under street lamps'
    golden arrows? There were mornings when I stared barbs
into your turned back, anchored you to everything ill-formed.
    Mama was in her beached boat staring into cloud-froth,
already gone—*Oracle, were the tulips the color of the dress*
    I would wear before leaving? Sometimes, knowing the future,

we can outrun it. I ran from your eyes' measure just short of the edge.
    Think of me as the baby destined to murder you.
Picture me on a hillside, winds toppling the cradle. Picture wolves,
    the gypsy's crystal darkening. *Oracle, does my father's*
hand still reach for my face? When you have it. A vision.
    Rock table, slowed pulse, frozen earth. Leave me there.

Cupid Enters
as the Love Primordial

Hey babe, let me tell you a story. Once the old forest,
its roots deeper than memory, was the where from which you

emerged—not banished from, but born. I drank the waters
of that place, drugged on vapor, foxfire, *ignis fatuus,*

and spoke something true. Then the air got thinner, the green
of the woods the green of fierce life—rhododendrons

on fire amid the rocks. It makes you weary, this aggressive
meadow, this tablet, the loud, screeching orgasm of everything

being made. Past canyons breeding winds in the bowls
of their valleys, out of stones that split to the root

and let out the darkness that was life.
That's right, babe: man emerges, blinking in the sudden light.

The mountain knows how to be patiently savage,
how to wait out the forms emerged from its mist. Singular

at first and then needing to couple, that's where I come
in. Bones gotta ache, legs gotta dance, even those

as burdened as bees, weighted with pollen. Then there
was no respite for humanity and its dramas, the play

never changing between acts. A climax, a stiff
bow, almost an apology. Truth is, you need me

more than ever. Where will you turn, the towers
broken and sifted to an earlier element, when you lift

your eyes to the skies above the Park and see only sky?
What will be promised when you turn back to the earth,

to its fucking, its fornicating, to the straining, generative
impulse, the flower penetrated by the bee? What we knew

first was sex, bed of dirt, that any stiff wind would get
you hard. So no fighting. No tears. Let me show you

my shaft. Let me show you the base of the world.

Zazu Recalls Psyche's Birth

For six years after I was born,
my grandmother would not speak to my mother.

Would not call me by my Christian name—Herald,
with an "e," as in "Hark! The Herald Angels Sing,"

a queer is born. Of course, no one knew that then.
Not even me. Mama, which is what we called

my grandmother, referred to me as "it"
for a season or two, flicking her narrow wrists

that were always bound in silver and bone.
Because I was not real yet, she said.

In Sierra Leone, where my grandmother is from,
babies are not named until the cord

drops off, curling in upon itself like a worm
in the sun. Mine was taken by doctors before a self

could take shape. Eventually though, I wore her down,
as I do, and she named me *Kohune wa.*

Great joy in her tongue. By the time Psyche found me—
although he wasn't her then, just a whip

of a boy, awkward in limb, ribs too large
for the body draped over them—I had left those names

long ago. *Joy* in St. Mary's on a bedstand.
Mama now a spot of shit the nurses

wished they could wash from the white
of the hospital sheets. *Herald* a wish that dried up

on my mother's tongue, along with all her other words
the day she found me with my uncle

in the backseat of his Coupe, my head resting
in his lap. My grandmother was right—

before we are what we are, we are nothing.
Zazu was a name the streets gave me.

An incantation or some other nonsense you speak
just before the canary bursts yellow and alive

from the thin air of your sleeve. The streets gave me
many names. Late spring of '64,

music was playing on a radio perched on a stoop
across the street from the Park.

It was the night they got me. Named me,
though the blow to the back of the head came first,

then the names—*Faggot, thicklips, freaky nigger bitch.*
Afterwards, I lay on my back, the stars

clearing the clouds at times, winking through
the city's glare. I couldn't see out of my left eye,

so I failed to notice when he stepped out
from behind the dumpster. Couldn't have been

more than fourteen, he pulled my head into his lap,
hummed along with the band playing live

from the Copacabana,
used his sleeve to soak the blood, the music

somewhere above us. That was the week
I started carrying a chain coiled in my purse,

an umbilical cord, toughened, *Bushmaster,*
because it would have to know how to bite.

The boy-who-was-not-Psyche was always at my side
by then. Since I had nothing else to teach,

I taught him the streets—the hard currencies
it minted. A way to manage, live off the dog food

in their shiny cars, drop a hairpin on the Avenue
without the badges seeing,

how to guard yourself. *You need a name, angel.*
Not that Sears & Roebuck number you have now.

Two days later, three in the morning, stripped
to his skivvies in a city fountain in the Bronx,

all the queens in attendance—
Gin and Martini then, Bethesda, Mama Sequins—

and baby didn't even flinch when I laid him back,
eyes open the entire time, like I taught him.

What shall we call her? Bethy asked.
Almond Butter? String Bean? Kitten Kaboodle?

No, I said, and I took my best shade
of Estée Lauder and wrote her name across

the paleness of the boy's chest.
Psyche? Fizzy said. *What kind of name?*

But *she* knew. Psyche knew. Sometimes
you have to name where it hurts.

We share that soul now, my half tough as gristle,
hers a cur backed into a corner and baring its teeth,

joined in an alley off W. 3rd, the cuss
of those fuckers still loose in the air, and my head resting

in her lap until I could manage myself again,
the noise in my chest. *Soul,* my sweetness!

Cupid Tells Psyche
about the First Time They Met

Man: Teach me how to make love to a woman
         with a heart condition.

Psyche: I thought I had been
            so discreet.

            I was over here last night
            throwing the furniture around.
            When you came in,
            I was thinking about how much
            I miss the sound of cicadas.

            On the farm we called them locusts—
            a plague, Cupid.

Man: Rough night?

Psyche: Two bucks for an hour, five
            for the night.

Man: When I first saw you,
         your long, white legs coming down
         Christopher, I looked up as you turned
         to look back, and it was over.

.

               I was carrying a chest-
      of-drawers for some bird I had met
      at the Algonquin. Dropped it square on my foot.

Fucking love, my toenail went black
as that horse named Unluckiness
I lost on the week before.

Why do you call me that name?
Cupid?

Psyche: It's what I call all of you.

Man: So there have been others?
I knew immediately what you were.
No surprises here. Never pulled the wool
on me. I like to think that from behind,
I can't tell a difference.

Psyche: Let's not speak of such things! Locusts!

Tell me the rest of the story of how we met.
The story I know that changes every time
you tell it.

Man: I lost the skin off my ass and a week's
pay to a horse named Painted Wing.
You were naked on the bed
when the radio hit the wall.
You never even flinched, gears
and dials raining down.

Tough luck? you asked.

The worst, I said.

Then you took a gear,
rolled the teeth along the underside
of my arm, my legs, my cock.

Psyche: I know about your girl
in that penthouse uptown. I know
about your daughter.
They don't breathe here. Only we do.

Man: We all got our "back homes."
I'm sure you got one too. Somewhere.

Psyche: Don't be cruel.

Man: Do you forgive me—
that other life, bringing you here?

Psyche: Never.

Man: Am I still your Cupid?

Psyche: Always.

II.

ONE LESS SOUL

(as told by The Golden Rats)

In the shadow of a parked car
or overpass, we are nothing but sound
to you—a wet gasp, a release.

In your weakest moments, you fear
you catch glimpses of us, naked on the bare earth,
a finger, nipple amid the gutter's trash.

You are not meant
to see our faces turned toward the sun,

our hunger for something so bright.
It's alright. It's already forgotten.

Without us,

how would you know what to grip
in the long night, in those far walks

you take down streets bisecting one place
of comfort from another?

What you crave of us is not touchable,
but a dream you turned away from,
a future too terrible to witness.

You try to imagine
what it must be like—flesh without certainty.

Is this our hands pressed to the gleaming of a blade?

Is this ourselves undressing for a stranger?
This is how we serve,

the act of our disappearing always
a relief to you. One less soul
to confound. One less body

to account for in the daylight world.

CUPID ATTENDS A SKIN FLICK

The exit's glare is like a warning,
and beneath its flush the usher, who let me in
despite my age, for the price of admission,
a smoke, and a hand slid under
the waistline of his trousers,
is like the effigy of some forgotten saint.
I realized early the world is a give
and take—an arrow with a barb
at either end.
             Back home, my mother
must be just now opening the oven door,
heat and the smell of rosemary fills the kitchen.
In the darkened den, my father snoozes,
a bristled walrus, the cold
of the TV climbing walls all around him.
I've often thought I could smother
a scream under the dust
my mother swabs from the backs
of furniture. Days in the bath,
I would masturbate for hours, over
and over, as gravity settled the house.

Once light is subtracted, what comes
to fill the dimness is sound and touch.
A thing, nearly religious, settles
under the domed roof with its stars
of falling plaster, and I can sense its space
solid as a man hidden in the dark.

Here, there is nothing
but texture and grain—burlap fabric of theater
seats, the chafe of denim and leather

as hands struggle with pockets. Nothing
of that sadness like a palpable noise,
the spent moment after every ecstasy.
                                    Above,
in his cabinet, the projectionist fumbles
with a cylinder of celluloid.
Pictures unwind from the spool
like parings of fruit lifted on a knife's edge.
We all know the way this begins.
We are familiar with the gist of rapture.
First comes the light, the flesh
follows after.

Mama's Chick'n'Rib

Table 5

"So was it a monster cock?" the sister asks.

Zazu orders steak and eggs, poached,
her lacquered nails clicking the tabletop.
Gin Phizzy says she isn't hungry, her meds
wetting the edge of need. A Coke
for her, and for Psyche—she'll have
the waffles. She likes the patterns
of the dish, straight lines surrounded
by a curving edge. Zazu is direct, points
a sharpened nail at Psyche.

"So tell us, love. Was it veined and gorged,
slim as a swizzle stick? Does the bulb of the head
make it look like a puppy? Was it more than
you could fit? Imagine. Did he break out the girl
in you?"
            Psyche can feel the heat at her throat.
"He was…fine. Gentle," she says.

Zazu and Phizzy laugh, tuck their heads
into their necks like hens in a rainstorm.

"I bet the girl doesn't know," Zazu says.

Phizzy nods back. Her hands shake around the curve
of her glass. "Queers don't do it with the lights on."

"You may have a monster on your hands."
Zazu sucks at a bit of meat between her teeth.
"A monster, and not even know it."

Psyche smiles. "Oh, honey. I know,"
she says with conviction, as if she believes.

Table 2

Tommy smiles as the windows begin to fog,
the lights outside becoming ghosts changing
garments. He knows Miss Crawford has turned up
the heat and AC, and the glass perspires, losing
its nature. Joan locks the doors, turns
the sign to "Closed." The place is packed.

Queens and rats from the Village nest into booths.
Across from him, Tommy's lover, Joe, grows
comfortable as they all become shadows
behind the pane.
                        Joe is off-duty,
his plainclothes making him seem less,
not like the mornings when Tommy watches
him rise, put on the blue law, and leave him.

For eight hours every day, Joe forgets
Tommy exists, his name never escaping
the thin space between his lips.
Tommy also knows Joe will take him
home tonight, peel off his clothes, fuck him.

He will be rough. He will hurt Tommy,
but even at sixteen Tommy knows
love can be made to resemble what it punishes.
Like the baton Joe once pressed
into Tommy's rectum, the wood cold
inside of him, Joe above him begging.

He takes Joe's hand, tries not to notice
the tremors. "What are you having?" he asks.
Joe looks up at him, the corners of his eyes
crosshatched with lines. "You," he says.

Tommy leans in as if to catch these words,
their lips brushing, and knows nothing could spook him—
not shade, not pain, surely not the lack of a name.

Table 23

The jukebox begins to play,
Martha and the Vandellas.
Zazu jumps from her seat, her nail file
a wand conducting her hips.

At table 23, Joan pushes sugar
into the palm of her hand, looks around.
He can tell by the change of light coming
through the window's condensation
it will soon be morning. Closing time.
Mama will just now be rising, putting on
one of her dresses—blue or black,
the only choices she knows.

Joan hears the jangle of bracelets
run the length of Zazu's arm, turns
to see her swaying to the music,
the music he has almost forgotten
in the after-hours rush, like the crystals
sequestered in his hand,
forgotten.
            The songs keep coming,
and others have joined Zazu.
Soon he will turn down the heat
and air. Let the windows clear.
Zazu twirls, a ballerina with hand
to hip and head, as if the gear
turning her were winding
down.
            Soon Joe will get up from table 2
and motion to Joan, who will pass round
the jars—one for tips, one for the register.
He will give Joe the precinct's cut

in a brown envelope. "Hush money,"
Joe will say and laugh, although
Joan will not.

Table 11

He feels sweat under his wedding band,
the solitary gentleman who sits at his booth,
the bulge of his belly pressed against
the table's Formica edge.
                              Joan takes his order,
asks no questions, for which he is grateful—
the man's gaze seemingly transfixed
by the cake stands and their bejeweled
contents—meringue, coconut, granulated
sugar.
        The crowd knows him as Brucer,
although that is not his name. They call
him *harmless, sweet,* yet none
have ever spoken to him. "I should charge
Brucie rent," Zazu says, "what with
the view he's getting of my ass."

The man orders coffee, black, the mug
warm against his palm. He thinks of chrysalises,
his parents' garden in back of a Brooklyn brownstone,
of being changed in those factories.

If he watched them long enough, the cocoons
would split. He thinks of those interiors,
soft and quiet, how it would be to take
one of these boys into that space, twined
together, coupled—that's the word he would use—
coupled into something beautiful and rare.

He watches Tommy bend at a table,
his shirt cut high enough to see Tommy's jeans
hang off the bone that cuts a V under the boy's ribs,
pointing the way to salvation.

The man sips his coffee, pictures his wife
warming her feet in the oven's open door,
waiting for him, patiently, as she does, as he
considers the route he'll use to get home.

The Floor

Zazu wraps an arm around Joan's
shoulder. Mouths the words
she knows by heart. They begin to kick
their heels, their platforms miming
the arched threshold of a doorway,
an exit. Gin Phizzy is passed out
in the booth, her eyelids trembling.
Psyche is signing Cupid's name
to the window, then drawing in a cock,
huge and bulbous.

Joan wishes it might never end,
but the jars go round, filling
with shekels, tubes of lipstick,
faux jewelry. When Mama comes
everything will be as she left it.
Her lips will thin when she sees the boys
in their ripped shirts, wrists limp
around their glasses. Joan will show her
money in the register, like a bed made
with many sheets, and she will clutch
her necklace, pearls as big as grapes.

Cheek-to-cheek, arm-in-arm,
intimate in this way, Zazu and Joan dance
as if outside in the gray rising
of the city there were nothing to fear—
no communism, no nukes nestled
in the foreskins of their silos,
no lily law or clenched fists,
familiar names printed on the third
page of the morning paper. Nothing
that cannot wait until the song is done.

Psyche Explains to a Young Man How to Gain Admittance to the Stonewall

First of all, honey, look the part.
Like you belong in a dive for queers.
You know what to do:
a sash of dahlia, dab of perfume.
                                    Think
floral in December, a winter garden.

The doorman, Blond Frankie, will ask you
to describe the inside of the bar—
entrapment being what it is, love.
                                    Lily law
rapping at the door like Poe's nevermore
raven. Nevermore? Please!

Here's what you'll tell Frankie:
                                    A void.
The walls bare, smoke-drenched
from the fire that nearly gutted the place.
Black paint they threw up over the soot.

A speakeasy without a note left in it.
Tell him about the bottles lit like churches
behind the bar, their fronts bearing strips
of paper with a name.

Not a word of how Zazu named
them all, giving them the monikers
of johns who had beaten her,
                                    pigs

who dragged her by her hair to the back
of their patrol cars—Patrick O'Reilly,
Danny Boy Schmidt, Lewis Tucker.

Tell him, you know it's $1.00 admission,
three for the weekend. Tell him the bar is a grotto—
just enough light to tell the mermen from
                                        flounders.
Don't mention the faces you miss: Arnie,
outed in the papers after a raid, found
in a bathtub, wrinkled, wrists not well.

Tell him you know Andy, the dancer,
but not a peep about the way your fingers
smell after you've slipped them past
his gold lamé trunks, wrapped a dollar
around the underside of his
                            balls.
Heaven, by the way.
                    Tell him you know
Maggie Jiggs, old personal friend, whose
pockets are most certainly not stuffed with
dope, acid, Desbutal.
                        Tell him you know
John, the bathroom attendant, who offers
you soap that smells like urinal cakes,
but who smiles and pretends not to
see the too many pairs of shoes in each stall.

Tell him you're aware the front room
is for whites, the back room for
                                blacks,
Puerto Ricans. Tell him you don't intend
any trouble.

Tell him about the wishing well
left over from when it was a Greek restaurant,
now used for storage. Leave out
how you tossed in a penny, heard it clang
against glass, ice buckets, whispered,

                              wished
for the hot number across the bar,
a night without a raid, or at least time enough
for Diana's song to finish playing.

Tell him jukebox, disco ball, sizzle
of sweat on the floor lights, the table
on which someone carved
                    REPRENT!

But don't ever tell him the real reasons
why you came. That your jaws ache
of love, your shoulders drawn up, tired.
Don't mention the blunt-eyed teenagers
you passed coming in, who may be doubling
back, their feet kicking at the gutter
for a pipe, a brick, and how you can't even
be bothered. Don't ask, if not here,

                              where?

Cupid in Black Spandex

I was a lost cause long before causes were the thing
to be had. At St. Pius—before I was expelled
for breaking the jaw of some wop

who called me queer, but never did a second time—
Sister Agnes told me that in the absence of light,
darkness rushes in, like the swift turning of a tide.
God's honest truth, she was wrong. It's money,

that filthy cockroach, that slips in
when the room goes dark. So we keep it dark here
at the Stonewall, and the money comes in to feed

on the trash of the place. Easy pickings as they say.
Most nights I sit here, papal prince of a church
that worships on its knees, too afraid to rise
and look me in the face. I've got the number

on all of them—Wall Street suits, five-star generals,
Princeton professors. If they've come in these doors,
they left marked with the scent of my piss on the hems

of their chinos. A simple recipe:
a room dark enough to create the illusion
of safety, a bright-eyed boy fresh off the streets
with a cock and a loud hunger,

and the prey of course. A blackmail racket,
extorting the city's elite was not a life I planned.
In my own youth, I was a wrestler,

TV celebrity. I needed a hook, so I shaved
my head, called myself The Skull. I was known
for my death-holds, my forearm pressed hard
to the throat's pulp. Funny word, *death-hold.*

Funny way to live. The word on the street
these days is that I've rubbed people out, former lovers
whose hands strayed into pockets I didn't give

them permission to pick. I won't weigh in on idle gossip,
but if it were true, I wouldn't mourn
a fucking one of them. Wouldn't miss catching sight
of their movements as they appeared in the door.

I've managed this shit-stain of a bar for more years
than I care to admit, and the money crawls in,
and if there's one thing I've learned it's that love—

whether you define it as grace or a hand job
in the backseat of a Buick—has a hefty tax.
But if you know how, you can lean
on the soft throat of that thing, press in until

you feel the airway give, until the eyes
go large, tear up, until they're ready to scream
for the love that's seated on their chest.

A Layman's Guide
to Cruising Greenwich Avenue

(as told by Zazu)

The trick is to be recognized
without being exposed.
It's all in the look, the strut.

You want them to see sex—
smoke rising from the stones
buried under your eyes, the thrust

of your hips navigating
the crooked thoroughfares.
Revlon says: *This is the year*

of wild frosted wines,
muddled golds. Hip-huggers
are revolution. The streets

don't lie. I can make a man
blush at fifty paces, his wife grasp
for his hand, but you'll need

one alone, a weakened
animal separated from the herd.
If he looks you sideways

as you pass, you've snared him.
The rest is just location, location.
Alleys will do in a pinch,

but the parks in summer
are best. You own part of that quiet,
it's a piece of you, like a bone

for balance in your inner ear.
Just don't get caught, sweetness.
Criminal is what they call it,

N.Y. Penal Code, section 240, 35,
subsection 4. Anyone found to be
wearing more than three pieces

of gender inappropriate
attire will be subject to criminal
treatment. Case you're wondering,

vestments caught around
your ankles count just as much.
I agree, it's indecent,

how every zipper begs to come
down, every button a wink.
Every thread has within it the start

of a tear. And when you've fallen
to pieces, you'll want to pick yourself
up again—panties, pants,

that silk that ties so neatly
in the front. But the next step
is most important. You will

look at him standing there,
holding his limp self, his pearls
already going cold on your wrist.

Now, love, turn and walk away.

CUPID BOTTOMS FOR PSYCHE

There is nothing you can bring to me that I cannot hold.
Broomsticks, candles, vases with oblong shapes, a rolled-
up skin rag, light-bulbs, soda cans, crowbars,

emery boards, a snapped-off table leg, jeweler's saws,
every form of vegetable life, umbrellas, desk lamps, a map.
There is room enough for the world inside me,
an entire cutlery set, defibrillator, prison survival kit:

cigarettes, six matches, flint, condoms, an empty syringe
with an eraser head over the tip, two bars of soap, Vaseline,
razor, eight ounces of marijuana, a Bible carved to fit a file.

My love, you cannot hurt me. I am no porcelain doll
to be broken. So get to it already—shuttlecocks,
hockey pucks, mallets, pool cues, clay pigeons, a pistol.
Nights at the baths, you learn how it's done,

how to open yourself to the new, and I swear baby,
you're the first. You're the only. And I can take it.
Whatever you have to give: pencil or candy cane,

garden snake or hose, bazooka, mushroom, twelve inches
of rainwater, twelve years of drought, a dozen curses
or disappointments, recriminations, the shit to your ankles,
a mother's kisses, tears, a father's love never earned,

never lost, doors closing, a brief, burning holocaust of love,
or sensation, violence, poverty, disease, that Fijian boy
found beaten and dead not a week after you fucked him

in back of the Cineplex, and shame, loneliness, spit
on your hands, on your cock, face, the warmth
on your skin just before the sun sets, what it feels like knowing
what you are, what they would call you if they saw,

what they would see inside if they could stand to look.
A mirror. A light. A brightness leaving your eyes, as it will,
as it does, as it always must once it's done.

THE WEDDING NIGHT

To some, vulgarity is a prayer we whisper to the bone
of our pelvis. Mine, honey, is tired of listening.

Above me, you switch off the light,
as you always do, afraid of what its touch could turn

you into, the reverse of some lupine curse.
We meet in the dark, sheets thick as thieves. I feel you

beside me, an absence overlaying omission, on your breath
the dark-reek of Chianti you slipped past the bellboy.

Your tongue is a wetted cork against my neck.
In the moments before light left us, you were

talking about your mother. How did you describe her?
A manacled tiger with a paper doll in its jaws?

A house cat eating its kittens under rosewood cabinets?
In the gloom, I trace what you won't let me touch

in the light, and your face under my fingers resembles
the scene of a Japanese screen, tight fabric, and under this

fog, stunted pines, crags, herons, fish scaled with jewelry,
and under this a woman naked, her garments strewn,

massaging the muscles of her leg. Your scar, run the length
of the right side of your face, is the texture of asphalt

on a summer day, bubbling tar at the moment it becomes
malleable. That first night you took me from the pier,

brought me to this blue motel with its lampshades
and scent of smoke and tallow, you wouldn't turn your cheek

to me. When I asked, you said it was a gift from your mother,
who was afraid men would be turned by the Osage dusk

of your beauty, so had held your face to the flames herself.
I let you enter me, and what you do know

is the rhythm of my body under yours, the hum that swells
in the back of my throat like a bee between the palms

of a boy. What you don't know is that after you
were asleep I struck the flint of a lighter and held it

over your face until I had memorized every trial
of its topography, until I was sure I knew you,

until the heat of the flint could be suffered no longer,
and I dropped the flame onto your chest. You woke

with a start, hurling yourself out of the bed, sweat
slicking your body, a tiny cherry between your breasts.

From this I learned two things. That there is a part
of you that will always be leaving me,

and there is nothing—maelstroms, moonlight,
the singeing mouth—I will not dare to keep you.

Psyche's Second Trial

I.

Everyone is here but you, Cupid:

Zazu, Gin Phizzy, Tommy, Martini Angel, Bambi,
that Puerto Rican boy with the crossed eyes and his lover,
the spitting image of a Botticelli Christ.

West End, the boy I have tried to tame,
the boy I found to replace you, complains of an itch
he cannot scratch.

The buildings lean in. Bambi says:
Girl, they've got salves for that shit at the clinic.

Zazu, with a squeal, pushes West End from her lap,
face-first into the gutter. *Oww,* she says. *VD is in the West End.*
Phizzy: *Notify the Centers for Disease Control.*
BC: *Pandemic!* West End comes up
grinning, his hair unspun straw.

This is the moment I would have taken
your hand, unnoticed by the crowds
dragging themselves toward the lights
just now coming on in the windows
along the street.
                    West End is pissing
against the side of an upscale hotel.

Since you left, I've been trying to forget you,
but at night when West End puts hands

against my body, their lightness
is not the same as yours.

West End zips his jeans. *Pandemic's right.*
I'll kill them all. Stop every heart
in a seven-block radius.

They'll never know what hit them.
Martini Angel lights a cigarette, calls out
to a passing sailor who refuses to look her in the eye.

I'll be lightning fast. West End takes a judo stance.
I'll be in your blood. You won't know what's hit you.

Gin Phizzy laughs. *Oh, girl. We never do.*

II.

Look. I have gold in my pocket, and West End
pulls aside the flap of his pants pocket, a tear in the seam
exposes the wooly bush of his pubic hair—

dirty blond and glistening in the lights of the hotel.
I smile at the familiar joke, the play of upset expectations.

When we arrive at the pier, the air is the scent
of wet metal, and I'm thinking of what West End told me
about his father's place,
upstate in the gut of iron country,
                                    God-fearing.
His father ran a scrapyard and on bright days
it was like a field of mirrors melting—

hubcaps, chrome fenders, hood ornaments West End
lined on a fence. When he told his father, hands
rubbed with grease, shoulders low, that he had made it
with a neighbor boy, his father slapped him so hard
his eye bled onto the grill of a Cadillac,

dandelions roaring soundlessly through the slats.
Leave. Don't come back.

Was he worth it? I ask. *The neighbor's boy?*

West End laughs. *Ah, son. They always are.*

III.

Along the waterfront of the Hudson, the empty trucks
on the loading docks are still, and West End
cat-struts through the silence, the hot, tight shade
of factory darkness. Across the river, the city glows.

I wonder at how far we've come from longing and desire
to arrive at the very same thing.
                              West End moves toward
the empty rigs, unburdened of their stock, the pump-
houses of tomatoes, peaches, heads of lettuce large as newborns.

He listens, then raps his fist on the doors,
the echo traveling all the way back.
                              From the inside,
the doors swing open—the scent of radishes and sweat
hits me like alcohol burning. A hand comes down, pulls West End
into the darker dark.
                    I hesitate.

Inside, men are pressed together like a stockyard slaughter,
some with jeans skinned
to their ankles. Everything is push, tug. Jerk, torque.

West End reaches one arm down, making a blade of his body,
drags me up. Body-to-body
with West End, the doors shut, and the last thing
I see is him.
     Then, just the din,
beasts in the ark's belly: hard, wetted, bristling,
hooves and shanks. The animal breathing.

I feel West End pushing on my shoulder, and I drop
in the darkness. My forehead rakes the stuttered
teeth of a zipper. I feel his cock. Take it.
Everywhere are invisible hands. West End is moaning,
and I grip the sound. I hear the cuss, the pining
of his ribs.
     Then voices from outside.

Police, the fucking lily law, are banging on the truck.
The doors jerk open and space will no longer hold
the frenzy. Push of what will not be contained,
what cannot be kept.
      I don't want to let go.
Outside is the river with its invitation. Its dirty innuendoes.
The city, a shut door. The loss
of so much. How each day dies again and again.

I run my fingers into that golden kink for a grip.
West End gasps. I whisper a message to you, Cupid,
into his navel. *Baby, don't go. Don't leave me.*

Lily Law jeers. *'Ey, faggots! Fun time's over.*

III.

Contemplating Infidelity, Poolside at the Local Y

It's here that you decide life is mere subtraction.
The clouds, hustling through the clear, thin at their lining,

like the stain of water on concrete gone to nothing.
On your towel, sunbathing, heat rises off of you

with some form of animal-nature. You will turn
it over in your mind, like a penny, bright and lucid,

dropped in chlorine, spun and gambled all the way
down. What will test your patience are the children.

You will not know them. They are neighbors,
browned, hair slicked, the knots of their enthusiasm

breaking the wake into spray. They will begin a game,
one you remember from youth as a lark, silly and juvenile,

therefore, important. One closes his eyes. *Marco,*
he says. *Polo*, says the others, just beyond his longing reach,

his fingers the most delicate and difficult of traps.
As in every game that is not adult, there will be a base—

some place of comfort beyond risk of what grasps
for us. One boy sits there, shivering, counting down

seconds before he'll have to leave the safety
of the ladder's rungs. *Three, two, one.* He's waist deep

now, parting the water, nearing the others he left
who are already over their heads and fighting. *You peeked.*

That's cheating. The boy from base touches the shoulder
of the nearest, his fingers intimate at the other's neck, feet

hooking each other, until the rules, broken, are remembered.
Marco, says the blind boy, treading. *Polo,* says the world.

Cupid at the Asylum

I had wounds sutured up the slope of my arms,
and they were like railroads, the hatch marks
you find on maps that lead to something.

Upon being committed to Atascadero State,
the Dachau for Queers, I was an aberrant mark
in the margins of the judge's book, a spider's

feast spinning on a single strand of web. Outside,
there are trees with oranges as big as human
hearts, and I don't think it's too much to ask

that God show a little mercy. What got me here
was an Italian dishwasher, the tattoos on his arms
faded, indecipherable stains. The wounds I got

from a plate glass window, running from the cops.
Folks glimpse stitches they think it's suicide,
a cry for help. I've lived long enough to know

there's no one listening. Why waste the breath?
What I remember is spotty, the electroshock making
my days slippery as eels. The orderly makes buzzing

noises whenever he turns off the lights.
I try to ignore him, but he knows I can feel current
in my bones. When I shut my eyes, I see my mother,

years ago, in a blue dress, bright clusters of cherries
gathered at the collar, her hand gripping mine.
We're waiting for something—a train, the songs

in Temple, my father to return from business.
It's been fourteen years, and we're still waiting.
The words the doctors are using now I can barely

understand—lobotomy, castration, sexual deviance.
The words are a part of a thing that's inside me
they say, a thing that will need to be lanced.

When the judge handed down the sentence,
ten years in Atascadero, I heard my mother cry out,
the dull thud of her body hitting the floor.

My mother did not come out of Dachau.
She came out of Auschwitz, though she never
spoke of it except to say when I was cruel

and would not eat, how in the camps
she'd consumed grass, said it was like eating
your own grave. I didn't know what she meant

until the night in the park when they caught us,
the dishwasher at my back and the scent of grass
strong in my nostrils, and then shouts, the lights,

and the knowing. The pills they give us here
make me feel like I'm buried up to my nose
in the earth's thickness. There's no coming back

from this place, and I can't help but notice
that my stitches pass over the very space where
the faded ink of my mother's number ascends

her arm, how my wound on her would obscure
the other. This of course has no meaning.
Crazy talk. The orderly, who brings creamed

corn and Jello, his teeth the same gray color
as the steak, asks what I intend to do
with my testicles once the doctors take them.

I tell him, send them to my mother.
Not to be cruel you understand, or snide,
or even indelicate, but because of all the people

in this world, she's the only one who would know
how to take madness and keep it. She's the only one
who would know what to do with such things.

PSYCHE IN THE TIME BETWEEN

The stone, as I remember, was eighty and seven paces
from the lee of my father's barn in northeast Nebraska.

Under that wedge of rock marooned in the meadow, I buried
my broken G.I. Joes, Captain Actions, Johnny Wests,

laid them, some naked, together, leg to joint, arm-in-severed-
arm, their stumps touched by black beetles, slug trails,

milk-soured skins of grubs. I grid the city in similar steps.
264 paces down Greenwich to 6th, 157 to Waverly Place

on the scripted edge of Washington Square. History
is often the horror of overturning what is kept

from light. Take the Park, a green expanse
where elms sweep the skies clean as blue gingham.

Once a swamp at the southern tip of Manhattan,
drained and made a pauper's graveyard, its foundation

the bodies of a cholera epidemic, 1798. Corpses
dumped into a common ditch—men, women, children,

elder and young alike made intimate. Picture them,
leg encircling neck, breasts pressed to lips,

groin to ass, no pulse save the few consigned
to death before the flutter of blood was still and stagnant.

What would time make of them? A broth, an unguent, a jelly?
A mattress stuffed with bones?

I'd like to think that this is what you and I have become,
but we are nothing so knitted or complex.

In the Park's northwest corner, I catch a glimpse
of a young thing leaning against the Hanging Elm.

Limbs groaning under the gravity of sin must be the same
sound that carries desire. The pause of my hand on the cup

of his ass. Oh, never mind. I forgot you dislike affection
in the light. Those soldiers could be there still,

the killing frost of a winter morning cauterizing
their severed points of connectedness. But let me tell you

how it all ended up. When the boneyard's lust
consumed ten thousand, the city converted

the grounds into a military display—cannons and heavy
artillery stacked upon a mesh of bones that could not

support it, the weapons collapsing into unmarked graves.
I have loved you all this time, and my heart has gone off

like a gun into the ground, wrapped in the arms
of the sinking masses. This is what it comes to—a gouged

trench into which everything is dropped. You call it death.
I call it desire. By the way, I made it with that boy, the slim

camber of his wrists a flute. He called me *querida, beleza.*
Darling, beautiful. Hope you don't mind, my love.

CUPID IN THE UNDERWORLD

It was all pointing the way of the inevitable:
bone-grit shore, expanse of gray water,

and the ferry with its trash heap of souls, used
as the last glimmer in the eyes of an addict.

When life left me, the other was inside me,
his desire a hot wind at my neck. Where has love

dumped us—without coin, without garment—
boy flesh, uncut, proportions mythic?

At the docks, there are so many of us, the arrow's
shaft still embedded in our stilled hearts.

Charon, in his robe and buckled life vest, rubs
thumb across fingers in a sign even the dead

recognize. The fare. I remember the game
once played with a cousin, a quarter hid in the folds

of the body, then challenged to find it. I searched
everywhere—under arms, tucked behind ears,

the obvious rectum—nothing. No precinct has gone
without plunder. I hold wide my hands,

track marks still visible, sign of the deficient.
Charon shoulders his scull, braces to embark.

None of you will ever know your worth
until you're standing on that final shore, the lantern

thinning, watching your last chance pull away.

The Witnesses of Love

I. Sunday, 7:02 a.m. Rain, Winds NE

Burglar hits Long Island. Mother of five loses
pearl inlay music box, rose and tulipwood design.
Plays Mozart's *Minuet* and *Turkish March*.
Box a gift from her mother, deceased, gassed
in Dachau. Police are worried. Woman refuses
to lock her doors. *I have nothing left,*
she says. *Let the bastards in.* Reward offered.

II. Monday, 4:48 p.m. Sunny and Warm. Humidity 25%

Hustler stabbed in heart and left in woman's
zinnias. Authorities rule dead on arrival. Elderly
woman mourns the ruin of her prize-winning flowers.
A man on scene remarks to reporters: *The boy had
the same mug as my son.* Police report: no motive known
at present. Man unavailable for further comment.

*III. Tuesday, 7:52 a.m. Hail and Sleet, Clear Skies Possible
    Later in the Day*

City Personals: SWM in search of Human or Other.
I'm fat, thick, 48, still have uncooked semolina
between my toes after a culinary-related accident in 1966.
I look like a hard-ridden Hoss on *Bonanza.* Either I strike
gold this time or I become a monk. Any takers?

IV. Wednesday, 3:47 a.m. Overcast, Wind Chill 25°F

African-American male walks unarmed into hospital.
Doctors are horrified. Upon being asked what happened,

he responds, *I was planting a garden when things got out of hand.* Police are suspicious and dusting for prints.

V. Thursday, 8:34 a.m. Early Morning, Dew Point 57°F

Homeless gentleman, seventy-five, cuts his hand
on an archery arrow while digging through trash
for food. Man fears, *I think I may be infected.*

VI. Friday, Midnight. Visibility Low, Fog Warning

Baby is found abandoned in a laundermat dryer,
still warm. Authorities demand answers of everyone.

VII. Saturday, 1:05 p.m. Partly Cloudy, Chance of Weather to Develop

Eyewitnesses report, *Love is real. I have seen it.*

Psyche's Third Trial

Run far enough, you run out of pavement.
Then you make do. You dig in your heels.

When we ran from the trucks, I carried
the scent of vegetable life in the grime

under my nails—could smell it oozing
from the bruises as they yellowed

around the edges. West End tripped.
The cops descended like bright-bellied

angels. I did not look back.
I heard he lost an eye.

Phizzy said he was beaten so badly
it was jelly by the time he reached St. Vincent's.

Since that night, I've been staying with Tommy.
I rarely go out, survive on a diet of sesame crackers

and tea. Week two of the shut-in, I gave up even that.
I wrote you letters, stuffed them into cracks

in the brick-face of buildings in the Village.
So much to tell. Gin Phizzy overdosed.

Bambi found her face down in a public toilet,
vomit pooled in her knock-off Chanel pumps.

You know the story. No one goes
to the Kew Gardens anymore. Vigilantes

have taken it over, running people out.
They've even begun to cut down trees,

threw stones at Tommy and his trick,
and Tommy said, *At least someone's*

getting their rocks off. I laughed,
though it hurts to do that.

People visit. Tell me I should get out.
I say, *If it was that easy, we'd all*

have plunged like rats off a burning ship
long ago. Fuckin' pigs raided the Checkerboard too,

the Tel-Star, even the Sewer. All of them
closed. Tamplona, the girl who lived with Tommy

over the Southside Butchery, went mainstream.
She's dating a secretary now, and Ricco

says every time he passes that queen
on the street, arm in arm with his girl,

he can't help but think of the time she spun
tampons into her locks like some blue-haired biddy.

That's how Tommy came up with her
real name. She goes by Stuart now.

I heard the secretary's pregnant.
Zazu's in prison—disorderly conduct.

Tommy's working in a hotel on Fire Island.
Even though you'll never read this, I have this hope

that if I fold the pages tight enough, the pulp
could become a seed. A pit that could

take root in the dirt of those cracks, send out roots,
break apart these streets.

ELEGY FOR JUDY

No one cares to see their star smoking in its crater.
It's the descent they want, to make their wishes,

and be done with you. On the radio today, I heard
news of your death, supine and dreaming upon

the bath's tile diamonds. At the Half Note Club,
Greenwich Village, I doubt you remember me,

poised as I was at the door in a crushed sequin
dress, hid behind smoke and my own ersatz

production. Judy, how can I tell you,
now that all the bulbs are broken glass, what

you meant to me, a cheap, lacquered bloom
rooted to a plot at the ass-end of the wind?

Rainbows can be deceiving. How many nights
did you parcel it in your hand, the blood orange

of Thorazine, Seconal, Ritalin as pale yellow
as those bricks scuffed by rubies? When I think

of your life, stood in the heat of the floor lamps,
it's not the harsh sizzle of your star falling

I tend toward. It's a story I once heard.
Mid-1950s, your career faltering like a dancer

in a spin, losing momentum, your feet dragging
from the weight of your heaviness.

In a room at the Four Seasons, hard
against the wall of mounting bills, your voice

cracking in the enameled acoustics of the shower,
you gathered about you your children—Liza, Joey,

serious Lorna—and clothed them in layer after layer
of garments, so you could slip from the hotel

without a case. Tomorrow, at your funeral, I will wear out
every dress I own—sequin, satin, crushed velvet,

polyester, gingham, I will curl a yellow rose
above my ear, and my shoes will be high enough

to make the risk worthwhile. A tornado touched
down in your hometown today, and I say, take

what you want, dear. Slippers, scarecrows, fresh linen
on a line, and that little dog too. Remembrance is a way

of loving, that gloved hand you lay upon cold stone,
emerald fields. Judy, my sister, you and I both know

it's loneliness hid behind that curtain, the twister
in the gut that picks us up, hurls us to heaven, the last

things we own rags upon our backs. So sing, baby.
Sing until that rainbow posits us somewhere over the rain

clouds, over the starlight, over the tangle and tatter
of America, and done with. When you left the club

that night, your last number still trembling the flames
in their colored globes, I touched your dress, the even

crossings of the threads a second skin against your hip.

Psyche Returns
from the Underworld

Yesterday, I sat on the fire escape,
watched the black kids in the building

across the way take a wrench to the hydrant
on the corner. One kid would yell, *Ho!*,

and they'd jump, putting all their weight onto
the handle, loosening inch by inch the bolt.

Once it gave, I swear it shot like a penny
from a gun. The kids began this shimmy

in and out of the spray, breaking it around
their shoulders, their hair soaking it up

till every 'fro nested jewels.
They laughed as if they'd discovered

some new rite not meant for the gods,
but for men—joyous and exalted.

Unbidden, they brought their lips close
and drank. I left the apartment then, went down

to the street. The sun hurt my eyes
it was so bright. I don't know if I can describe it,

how when I touched the wet concrete, the taste
there was the city, huge and noisy. My city!

A girl playing hopscotch through the spray
stopped when she saw me, my fingers still

resting on my tongue. *Are you a boy
or a girl?* she asked. *Honey,* I said,

touching her face, *I am both.*

Cupid in Sheep's Clothing

I was never the kid to finish first. Nor was I
a wonder on the field, or a murderer of skirts.

I was blessed like most in this city—a life
and not much more promised. To the east,

where my baby sleeps, southside of the Bronx,
his fingers pressed to the pulse of my wife's neck,

he is healthy. The world outside only noise,
racket of sirens, trucks, the winos loud

in their failures. As I approach the Stonewall, I think
about what it takes to keep him safe.

When he was born, the doctor took one look
at his flat face, small chin, and said it was Down's.

My wife will not let me touch her, not since
I suggested we give it up, an albatross I called him,

though I have since changed my mind.
Is one moment of doubt unforgiveable treason?

Something impossible to make right?
Outside the bar, a group of queers are gathered,

their faces slick from the heat, and it's as if their sin
is leaking out of them, every inch of their bodies crying

out against God, against nature, a skim of sleaze
that they leave on the sidewalks, in the sheets

of their rooms where they do things heaven turns
away from. Dressed in plainclothes, badge heavy

in my front breast pocket, I tell myself that I have no
part of the shit and scum of this place. As I pass

one of their number, a Puerto Rican with hair the texture
of steel wool whistles, prances over and places

a hand on my stomach. I let him touch me.
After my boy came home, Father Sullivan said to me,

the confessional screen between us, the Holy Father
gives each man his cross, to test what he's made of.

Across the street, my superior and the other deputies wait.
All that's needed is my signal and hell begins

for the ones who deserve it. At his Baptism in St. Peter's,
the sanctity wetting his forelocks, his skin the scent

of almonds, I made myself swear there was nothing
I wouldn't sacrifice to promise him a world better

than the one I saw every day, the girls cold with syringes
in their arms, the degenerates catcalling their filth,

spics and Jews taking every opportunity.
At the door to the bar, the bouncer sizes me up,

but I've been schooled in what to say, how to play.
Inside I feel the darkness reach for me, the men corralled

into corners, hands finding darker places. What makes
them think they can reach for whatever they want?

There's a need starts in my knuckles, moves
up through my arm. This must be the feeling Abraham

had on that peak overlooking the Cities of the Plain
as God made clear his plans to rub them out.

He must have felt something like grace, spared
when so many others went to nothing, and how

must that grace have tasted when God
later demanded his son? There are none

of the righteous here, and I would hold the brand
to the fire that would burn this place clean,

the ashes gathered and buried so the ground itself
could forget forever the stories held here.

One day my son will walk the world that I give him,
and the gutter's contents will speak of the father

I have been. Soon I will give signal for the raid to start,
and the cleaning will begin, the patrons herded

into the riot cars, and the first I will take will be
the grease bag outside. When my hands

touch him, he'll know who the powerless really are.
This is my gift for my son, my life, to do with

what he will—suckle it, sharpen it, build a home,
a cross out of the wind, nails, wood, and rope,

to hang it from his neck.

IV.

Psyche's Fourth Trial

We had no memory of it, the pitch,
                              the toss,
the feeling of falling even as we ascend.
There was nothing special about that night, no gods
        with their strong hands
parting the clouds, or Judy now singing on her thunderhead

in the rising smoke, her wings spread azure, ozone,
        color of bluebirds.

So how to explain it, falling that was flying, lift that was loss?
If I look behind me, I'll see my adolescent self
                              standing in my father's fields,
the far edge lit by wildfires, the noise like the hiss
of a congregation. Father is yelling, calling for water
        never to come,
                        as if they meant it when they told us,
Ask, and you shall receive.

                Mama's grinning, her face
a dishrag caught fire, her hand a prayer on my shoulder.
I will not look back at this, at an undoing
that rages too close, house and barn
                              threatened, the horses screaming,
Mama whispering beside me, *This is how hell
arrives, low, undaunted.*

                Gods help us, how could any of us turn
as our collective fathers beat at the earth now ashed?

I remember Granny saying, *Fire is fallow.*
Sometimes you have to burn the seed to make it grow.

Perhaps we should have looked back
before we pitched ourselves forward.
Better to be salt.
Better to be a note left hanging in the air.

Psyche Incites a Riot

This I brought upon myself.
All of us, newly returned
from the edge of the underworld,
the body going under, but not the voice.
You know the story, the flags
of Fire Island hung at half-mast.
When the swine came, their boots
blackened, buckles spit-shined
until they flared under the naked
bulbs, it was us that were corralled.
No cowboys with their silver
guns, angel hands, were there
to keep the peace. Zazu, as she
is cuffed and led away, sings
"Hello Bluebird" and the girls
with their manhood tucked
and taped, mouth the echo.
We are constituted by an absence
of voice, a lust for tenor. Grief
is the thickest of greases,
and what it covers is clay and steel,
graffiti, a faint penny taste
in our mouths. We have bitten
our tongues like raw mothers,
we have birthed ourselves, hemmed
by everything we have borne.
The veils have been pulled
from our faces, and we are
using them as shields.

THE SIEGE

They didn't think we had it in us,
the balls. *Faggots are revolting,*
but not riotous, they said.
Except in the muddle
of their sexes. We had nowhere left

to go, and it seemed that whatever
came to our hands was leaving.
Outside the bar, under the full face
of the moon, the night was so humid
we felt as slicked and oiled

as baseball gloves. The mythic
possibilities of that hour
were endless. Fairies of every color
throwing glitter at the walls
of Jericho. It's in the nature of things

to come to ruin. When your face—
and it's always your face—is pressed
into asphalt, the abrading grit
of brick and cement, the smell
you come away with is smoke,

powder, brimstone. I was not
the first to hurl coin at the thieves,
as if someone had decided this
is what they wanted of us. I was not
the first to pick up bottles with

the purpose of unmaking them, nor
wave the parking meter like some
wand that could conduct history.
But watching the prisoners roughly
shoved into the wagons, their wigs

ripped away from them, faces
bleeding, the catcalls started—
Gay power! Gay power!
as if we had turned the trick.
Hip-tilt, moon-bashed, joy.

Cupid as a Folk Singer
Consorting with Violence

Once the windows shattered like a misplayed
    note, the door warped, we knew
        we were coming out of hell. You could

feel the touch of night air from the bay,
    and it was balm, dissolving that film
        of shame on our faces. The pigs, penned

in the bar, squealed as the dagger came
    closer, their pistols gripped like loved ones.
        Looking around, we were birds singing,

pulling out plumage for arrows, tangling
    our beaks with death. And it was something
        akin to death that came for me. One officer

leapt into the melee, and seized me by
    the waist, pulling me downward and back
        into the dim interior. Once inside, they

gathered round me, incensed. The first blow
    was the hardest. I remember my fingers
        on the strings, the caress of the bow,

the catguts' lick and vibration. Then *snap*.
    The string cutting into me, as if the gods
        demanded hemorrhage of their favors.

So when the second blow came, it was
    like barter. I will give you the body
        for this song, the drum thump of flesh

on flesh, the jangle of glass falling, sirens
        in the distance, the whoosh of fire taking.
                My eyes, swollen to slits, cracks around

the door, saw the flames loot the wood
        and brick, the plastic frame of the window
                melting and dripping like wax.

I Heard They Were Queer for One Another

The police were boxed inside the Stonewall once the crowd
turned, shifted its hips and cut with their collective eyes.

I heard the mood changed outfits. Queens calling out the girls
escorted from the bar: *Have a good rest!*

Those bags under her eyes have been packed for weeks!
Waving them off. *Bon voyage!* Then a thing happened no one's

quite sure of, but I can only assume it began as a stirring
of something in the crotches of the blue boys,

as the queens batted their lashes like they wanted it hard
and the blue were happy to oblige.

The tide turned so suddenly, some heavenly lifeguard
absent from his post, and the rains began—first pennies,

then nickels, dimes, quarters, the economic escalation
of violence, till the queens minted stranger currencies,

bricks, curses, fire. I heard it happened in the Stonewall,
the doors locked, the police huddled together. Heard it started

with the stroking of a holster, a rookie talking dirty
to the bar's only exit that had turned as catty as a bitch decked

to the nines in a heat wave. I heard they stood close enough
to kiss during the worst of it, wetted their lips and stared

into each other's eyes. How they wanted to say things.
Talk about their wives and children, their guns, their cocks.

I heard they felt each other tremble as the window
shattered, moved closer as the floor shuddered

with each thrust of something on the door. Then the flame
took and they were in a moment one breathing, sweating animal,

red-hot with life in its belly. They heard the orders
of their superior—*Nobody fire! Help is coming!*

They thought about what it meant to do this together, to stand
shoulder to shoulder, their guns half-raised in a circle jerk

right out of nightmares, the fairies now tigers, bottom now top,
cocktails burning, and I heard it was the queerest thing.

Cupid Wakes from a Bender to Witness Psyche at the End of Her Trials

When I woke, the night was long birthed and walking
the streets, and the first thing I perceived was my foot

in the piss trail of light from the lamps on Christopher,
my back friendly with the brick-face of a wall.
What I heard then was new and alien. Not the sirens,

those old divas wailing. Not the alley's catcalls,
the ping of a bottle dropped, the shouts, the curses,

which were nothing unique. It was the awe between
these sounds, like the breathing of someone hidden
who wants to be found. I stood then, stepped into the street.

No one noticed. I stood there, the crowd
swelling in front of the Stonewall like a struck eye,

the night going purple to old yellow in the margins
of the streetlamps. I remembered thinking
someone must be dead, another of us found snuffed,

the song captured in some boy's throat as it tried to rise.
Then I saw you, heels in your hand and an arrow

in your side like a St. Sebastian tied to his stake,
or at least the spirit of the icon was there, a kind
of swooning in the face of so much rising.

Everything goes tipsy after this and riots make
their own time. Afterwards only slices you remember,

a boy with blood on his neck, shirt balled and pressed
to his lip. The weight of someone's body you caught
as they tripped. There's no way to own a thing like that,

even though I knew I would spend the rest of the long ages
claiming that I touched you, and that this was more

than something I had failed. Years later, I'll say
that I fought by your side, your hand gripped in mine,
even though it was someone else's you held.

My beautiful brawler, I saw when you fell.
You and the other girls who rolled up your pants

into knickers, formed a kick line. When the police
charged, you turned a step too late, and I watched
you hit your knees from the force of the blow to your back.

Lifetimes from now, I'll want to name myself your savior,
but it was one of your kind, a street kid, who took your hand

and pulled you back into their number. Me, I was the one
who watched all of your trials—suffering in the face
of my desire for the grit of your jaw, brace of your back—

did nothing but wait for the story to finish.

SHRINE OF HUMAN FACES

At first, I imagined you searching
as I was searching. Imagined us passing
in the crossing of two streets,
your shoulder brushing mine,

me looking off
into the high branches of the Park,
toward some future that I imagined
had us pinned to a tableau of stars.

Whoever said those suns were anything
more than beautiful, burning rubbish?

How Queens Lose Their Looks

How strange it is to be unafraid. To learn that in the aftermath
of violence there is beauty, windows recut into sapphires,

polish of wet charcoal, the solemn smoking embers.
When the riot trucks left, gave up the street to the dawn,

we walked out again, those who had not been taken
by the raid, all of us nursing wounds of one kind or another,

black eyes, a broken nail, the sculpted nothing left in the place
of so much pain. It wasn't exactly nothing though.

Our lives not entirely undressed. Zazu couldn't stop grinning,
her cheek swollen. Tommy kept repeating: *Scandalous!*

Did you see them running? Did you see them shit their pants?
This must be what it's like—the sacrifice paid, the blood dried,

flaking, the blade still wet, and the faces of the exalted,
the ones left after, feverish, their limbs still itching with it all.

We walked as if dazed, drugged, our feet finding familiar paths,
the circuit of the park, the Square, looping back always

past the gutted ruin of the Stonewall, the smoke still rising
like a thought bubble in a comic, what you could read

on everyone's face printed there. What our lips couldn't form.
The Stonewall is gone! The STONE WALL is gone!

No one could stand still, so we walked on past the window
dressings and marquees, the headlines newly inked,

past silence loitering on the Saturday-morning streets,
and the officers patrolling, eyeing us up and down, swinging

their sticks. There we were in that new city. There we were
strolling our avenue, none of us dropping our eyes to our feet.

PSYCHE DEIFIED

Dress of violet, heels high above
the glitter of glass, I have again
made of myself something new.
It was always my hands I hated
the most, the way they betrayed
with their girth and coarseness.
I tried everything—lotions, creams,
salves, liniments. Still as hard
and heavy as irons. Is this why
you hate me? Because you see
in me both yourself and your desire? I too
cringe when the door to the dressing
room is thrown open, exposing
the ruse and the rouge, the mown
stubble like a shadow under the base.
No one likes the death of illusion.
Now, there is nothing to be sure
of, no absolutes, no angels in
the drag of sanctity pointing
the way to heaven. But if you
were me, the hand coming
for your mud mask, and you unsure
if under it was godhead or mortal
decay, wouldn't you recoil—
like a pubic hair wound tighter
than history's noose?
                              I know your
bedtime stories, and I know my own.
So when the story came for me that night,
with its clubs hard as cocks, its leather
rubbed to shine, all I could hear
was your voice, talking of love,

making the ending sound easy,
ardor tucked into its purse, but me—
I was never quite sure if it were a heart
or a brick I fondled. Whatever it was,
whetstone or gold standard,
a box containing the darkest of beauty,
I was not able to contain it.

NOTES

"The Golden Rats": This poem and others in the collection were inspired by a handbill written and distributed by Thomas Lanigan-Schmidt, a participant in the Stonewall Riots.

"Mama's Chick'N'Rib": The title refers to an eatery on Charles Street in New York City, which became a gay hangout during the 1960s.

"Psyche Explains to a Young Man How to Gain Admittance to the Stonewall": The reference to the bottles bearing strips of paper on their fronts refers to a common practice of gay bars in New York at this time. Bars could not legally sell liquor to known homosexuals. To get around this law, gay bars were often run under the ruse of being bottle clubs, establishments that allowed members to bring in bottles of liquor and leave them at the bar with their names printed across the labels. Waiters at such clubs could pour members drinks from their private stock. At the Stonewall, however, the names on the bottles were fictitious, and in practice the club sold drinks to anyone the doormen admitted.

"Cupid in Black Spandex": The poem's point-of-view is that of Ed Murphy, aka The Skull, who came to be a manager at the Stonewall Inn and who allegedly ran a blackmail ring that preyed on the bar's patrons.

"Cupid Bottoms for Psyche": The inspiration for this poem came in part from the entry "14 Unusual Objects Removed from Men's Rectums in Hospital Emergency Rooms" found in *The Gay Book of Lists* by Leigh W. Rutledge (Alyson Books, 2003).

"Elegy for Judy": Judy Garland died on June 22, 1969. Allegedly, on the day of Judy Garland's death, a tornado touched down in Kansas. In some versions of the story, the tornado was said to have touched down in Garland's hometown, which is untrue, seeing as Garland was born in Grand Rapids, Minnesota. No doubt the story in fact alludes to the hometown of Garland's most famous film character, Dorothy Gale.

"Cupid as a Folk Singer Consorting with Violence": The title's speaker is loosely based on Dave Van Ronk, a prominent folksinger involved in the Stonewall Riots.

Acknowledgments

Grateful acknowledgment is made to the periodicals in which the following poems first appeared, sometimes in slightly different form.

Arcadia: "Contemplating Infidelity, Poolside at the Local Y"

Bluestem: "Suitors Mark the Arrival of Psyche on Christopher Street," "Zazu Recalls Psyche's Birth," "Cupid at the Asylum," and "Psyche in the Time Between"

Crab Creek Review: "Psyche Returns from the Underworld"

North American Review: "The Siege" and "I Heard They Were Queer for One Another"

Prairie Schooner: "Two Falsehoods," "Psyche Explains to a Young Man How to Gain Admittance to the Stonewall," "How Queens Lose Their Looks," "Cupid Attends a Skin Flick" as "Cupid's Study," "Elegy for Judy," and "Psyche's First Trial"

The Spoon River Poetry Review: "Cupid in the Underworld," "The Wedding Night," and "Psyche Incites a Riot"

"Cupid as a Folk Singer Consorting with Violence" as "The Folk Singer's Fall" was included in *Outscape: Writings on Fences and Frontiers*, edited by Jessie Janeshek and Jesse Graves (Knoxville Writer's Guild, 2008).

The author would like to give special thanks to the author David Carter, whose book *Stonewall: The Riots that Sparked the Gay Revolution* served as inspiration for many of the poems in this collection.

For the guidance, friendship, and encouragement over the years during which these poems were written, I would like to express my deep gratitude to Charlotte Pence, Arthur Smith, Marie Howe, and Marilyn Kallet.

The author is also especially grateful to Nebraska Wesleyan University and the University of Tennessee for their support.

A thank you as well goes to Peter Campion for choosing this collection for the Trio Award, but more importantly, for believing in these stories. Thanks also to all the people at Trio House who put in the work and were so gracious and professional while doing so.

A special acknowledgment to Erika Schukraft Terl, who asked the question, why haven't these histories been told?

—

And finally, for Chris…for teaching me what defines a marriage, and then helping me make one.

About the Author

Bradford Tice is a poet and fiction writer who currently teaches at Nebraska Wesleyan University. His first book of poems, *Rare Earth* (New Rivers Press), was awarded the 2011 Many Voices Project and was named a 2014 Debut-litzer finalist. His work has also appeared in such periodicals as *The Atlantic Monthly, North American Review, The American Scholar, Alaska Quarterly Review, Mississippi Review, Epoch,* as well as in *Best American Short Stories 2008.* He is also the winner of *Prairie Schooner's* 2009 Edward Stanley Award for poetry.

About the Artist

Ronnie Beets was born in Fortaleza, Brazil and adopted as an infant by a family in East Tennessee. Many of his paintings exude the undeniable influences of Cubist and Abstract masters like Picasso and Chagall while remaining boldly unique. His subject of choice is the human form and portraiture, but his ever-growing body of work covers a broad spectrum of styles from pure abstraction to stylized realism. Ronnie has exhibited extensively throughout the Southeast and has been well received since relocating to Atlanta, regularly showing in a variety of venues around the city. His work hangs in numerous collections across the United States and overseas. He is currently working on opening a gallery in Atlanta that highlights the work of inner city youth and other artists who may not have the resources, support, or even the simple encouragement to pursue a career as a professional artist. His work can be seen on his website: www.aRtBeets.com and @aRtBeets on Instagram, Facebook, Tumblr, and Twitter.

About the Book

What the Night Numbered was designed at Trio House Press through the collaboration of:

Matt Mauch, Lead Editor
Sara Lefsyk, Supporting Editor
Ronnie Beets, Cover Art
Dorinda Wegener, Cover Design
Lea Deschenes, Interior Design

The text is set in Adobe Caslon Pro.

The publication of this book is made possible, whole or in part, by the generous support of the following individuals and/or agencies:

Anonymous

About the Press

Trio House Press is a collective press. Individuals within our organization come together and are motivated by the primary shared goal of publishing distinct American voices in poetry. All THP published poets must agree to serve as Collective Members of the Trio House Press for twenty-four months after publication in order to assist with the press and bring more Trio books into print. Award winners and published poets must serve on one of four committees: Production and Design, Distribution and Sales, Educational Development, or Fundraising and Marketing. Our Collective Members reside in cities from New York to San Francisco.

Trio House Press adheres to and supports all ethical standards and guidelines outlined by the CLMP.

The Editors of Trio House Press would like to thank Peter Campion.

Trio House Press, Inc. is dedicated to the promotion of poetry as literary art, which enhances the human experience and its culture. We contribute in an innovative and distinct way to American Poetry by publishing emerging and established poets, providing educational materials, and fostering the artistic process of writing poetry. For further information, or to consider making a donation to Trio House Press, please visit us online at: www.triohousepress.org.

Other Trio House Press Books you might enjoy:

The Alchemy of My Mortal Form by Sandy Longhorn
  2014 Louise Bogan Winner selected by Carol Frost

Your Immaculate Heart by Annmarie O'Connell, 2014

Flight of August by Lawrence Eby
  2013 Louise Bogan Winner selected by Joan Houlihan

The Consolations by John W. Evans
  2013 Trio Award Winner selected by Mihaela Moscaliuc

Fellow Odd Fellow by Steven Riel, 2013

Clay by David Groff
  2012 Louise Bogan Winner selected by Michael Waters

Gold Passage by Iris Jamahl Dunkle
  2012 Trio Award Winner selected by Ross Gay

If You're Lucky Is a Theory of Mine by Matt Mauch, 2012

CPSIA information can be obtained at www.ICGtesting.com
Printed in the USA
LVOW12s0248070315

429474LV00004B/7/P